LIFE IN A
PLAINS CAMP

© Tom Lovell

Bobbie Kalman

Crabtree Publishing Company

www.crabtreebooks.com

LIFE IN A PLAINS CAMP

Created by Bobbie Kalman

(Dedicated by Deanna Brady)
For Jackie, T.J., and Alberta

Author and Editor-in-Chief
Bobbie Kalman

Researchers
Deanna Brady
Kate Calder

Project editor
Deanna Brady

Copy editors
Heather Fitzpatrick
Kathryn Smithyman

Computer and Graphic design
Kymberley McKee Murphy

Production coordinator
Heather Fitzpatrick

Consultants
Deanna Brady, Corporate Board Director, PHO2000 American Indian Outreach Programs; American Indian Changing Spirits
Professor J.S. Milloy, The Frost Centre for Canadian and Native Studies, Trent University

Photographs and reproductions
The Greenwich Workshop, Inc., Shelton, CT:
James Bama: *A Mountain Ute* (detail), page 18
Tom Lovell: *The Gift* (detail), 1, 26; *Trading at Pecos Pueblo, About 1500* (detail), 4; *The Iron Shirt* (detail), 6, back cover; *The Finishing Touch* (detail), 8; *The Wolf Men* (detail), 22; *The Vision Seeker* (detail), 30
Howard Terpning: front cover, *Old Country Buffet: The Feast* (detail); *Blackfeet Storyteller* (detail), 9; *The Talking Robe* (detail), 16; *Shield of Her Husband* (detail), 20; *Pride of the Cheyenne* (detail), 25; *Passing into Womanhood* (detail), 27
Sherry Harrington, page 24 (left)
© permission of Lewis Parker, page 23 (top)
© permission of Lazare & Parker, page 12
Alfredo Rodriguez, page 21
Smithsonian American Art Museum, Washington, DC/Art Resource, NY: George Catlin, *Ball Play of the Choctaw—Ball Up* (detail), page 29
© Craig Tennant, pages 14, 25 (bottom), 26 (bottom), 27 (bottom)

Illustrations
Barbara Bedell: pages 5, 7 (left), 19 (top left, bottom), 28 (top)
Margaret Amy Reiach: hide background, pages 6, 7 (right), 8, 9, 14 (insets), 15, 17, 18, 19 (top right), 20, 24 (right), 28 (bottom)
Bonna Rouse: page 4 (top)

Crabtree Publishing Company

www.crabtreebooks.com   1-800-387-7650

PMB16A	612 Welland Ave.	73 Lime Walk
350 Fifth Ave.	St. Catharines	Headington
Suite 3308	Ontario	Oxford
New York, NY	Canada	OX3 7AD
10118	L2M 5V6	United Kingdom

Cataloging in Publication Data
Kalman, Bobbie
    Life in a Plains camp / Bobbie Kalman.
        p. cm. -- (Native nations of North America)
    Includes index.
    ISBN 0-7787-0369-X (RLB) -- ISBN 0-7787-0461-0 (pbk.)
    This book introduces children to the traditional daily life of the Native people who lived on the Great Plains of North America.
        1. Indians of North America--Great Plains--Juvenile literature.
    [1. Indians of North America--Great Plains.] I. Title. II. Series.
    E78.G73 K36 2001
    978'.00497--dc21

                                                LC2001017295
                                                CIP

CONTENTS

PEOPLE OF THE PLAINS

The Great Plains cover the central area of the North American continent.

The Great Plains region is a huge area that stretches east to the Great Lakes, west to the Rocky Mountains, north to the Canadian prairie provinces, and south to Oklahoma, Texas, and Mexico. Centuries ago it was a vast sea of grass edged with woodlands, rolling hills, and the foothills of huge mountains. Most of this central region is flat and lacks trees and edible plants. Winters can be freezing cold, and summers scorching hot. Before Europeans arrived, more than thirty Native **nations** lived on the Great Plains, including the Blackfeet, Assiniboine, Mandan, Cree, Sioux, Crow, Cheyenne, and Comanche.

Many nations followed the giant herds of buffalo that roamed the Plains. These people lived in camps that could be put up and taken down quickly and easily. Above, these Apaches of the Southern Plains have set up camp to trade buffalo hides for corn and pumpkins grown by southwestern Pueblo farmers.

Different languages and cultures

The many Native nations who lived in camps on the Plains shared a similar way of life. They hunted buffalo as their main source of food and made their homes using buffalo hides, but their customs and styles of dress were very different. Their languages were also unique to each nation.

Relying on dogs

Before explorers and settlers brought horses to North America, the Native people had no horses. They traveled over land on foot and used dogs to help carry their supplies. They strapped their tent poles over a dog's shoulders to make a carrier that the French traders called a *travois*. Supplies were attached to the poles to be dragged along by the dog.

Horses on the plains

In the 1600s, Europeans arrived in North America and brought horses with them. Some of the horses escaped into the wild and were caught and tamed by Native people, who became skilled riders.

Horses changed the way of life of the Native people. Using horses, people could follow the buffalo when they moved from one place to another with the seasons. People who were farmers became more **nomadic** because hunting buffalo on horseback was much easier than hunting on foot.

(above) Traveling on foot was slow and tiring. A family could walk only a few miles a day, and the dogs could pull no more than 50 pounds (23 kg) of supplies.

© Tom Lovell

Plains camps consisted of tents called **tipis**. Each tipi was the **lodge**, or home, of one family. The word tipi is a Dakota word meaning "place where one lives." Tipis were temporary homes that suited the nomadic lifestyle on the plains. These lightweight, cone-shaped homes could be assembled and moved easily. They were made of long, thin wooden poles and covered with buffalo hides. Covering a small tipi required about twelve hides, and larger ones, as many as fifty. A Plains camp had both large and small tipis. The size of the tipi depended on the wealth of the family.

In summer, the bottom of the tipi cover was raised for ventilation, as shown in the picture. In winter it was fastened down tightly to hold in heat, and people packed snow or dirt around the bottom to keep out cold drafts. They also put an extra lining of hides on the inside of the tipi for warmth. The air moved up between the inner and outer layers of hides, helping smoke from the fire escape out the top. Long poles were used to open the flaps at the top of the tipi, allowing smoke to drift out directly above the fire as well. The flaps were closed when it rained.

PUTTING UP A TIPI

The camp was set up in a circle with an opening on the east side of the circle. The chief set up his tipi opposite the opening, and the others set up near him in order of importance.

At night, buffalo-hide "beds" circled the fire. Smoke from the fire drifted out of the opening at the top of the tipi.

Tipis belonged to the women of the camp, and they set them up at each site. To form a frame for the tipi, three or four poles are pulled together and tied at the top. They are then raised upright to create a cone shape.

Several poles are added to the frame to fill in the gaps. Each is leaned up against the central notch.

The tipi cover is attached to the last pole. The pole is lifted upright and leaned onto the rest of the frame at the back of the tipi.

The cover is unfolded around the framework of poles. The doorway is created where the cover comes together. It often faces east towards the rising sun.

FAMILIES AND CLANS

Groups of families lived together in a camp. They cared for and respected one another and shared their food or supplies. They felt a strong connection, not only to their family members, but also to their **ancestors**.

Clans

Some nations were subdivided into large **clans**. A clan included family members who were related by a common ancestor. Because they were related, men and women of the same clan often were not allowed to marry one another.

Husbands and wives

In many camps, a man was required to obtain several horses before he was considered able to support a wife. Once married, the husband and wife shared the work of the family, but the wife took care of everything in her home. She did not take her husband's name.

Children

Children were valued greatly. Young brothers and sisters played together, and their older siblings looked after them. As children became young adults, boys protected their sisters, and girls made moccasins for their brothers, but they spent most of their time with friends and relatives of the same gender.

Women took pride in the appearance of their husbands. They made their clothing, braided their hair, and adorned their outfits with decorations of porcupine quills and beads. This young wife adjusts her husband's bear-claw necklace before a celebration.

© Tom Lovell

Elder and wiser

Elders were senior members of the Plains society who acted as advisers to people in the camp. Family members went to them for guidance. Elders also knew the old stories that had been handed down through families and nations. They taught the stories to the children of the camp. In those days, Native people did not have a written language, so stories were used to teach values, history, rules, and codes of behavior. They were told over and over so people would remember them. Elders also taught children the skills they needed as adults and helped them pass from childhood into adulthood.

This Blackfeet elder keeps his listeners fascinated with a legend about a buffalo and beaver. Children learned valuable lessons from stories about animals.

9

THE CAMP SOCIETY

Bands were made up of several families of the same nation, or tribe, who generally camped together. The sizes of bands varied. They had to be large enough to provide protection for their members and small enough so the hunters could feed everyone in their camp. In summer, groups of bands assembled on the plains to visit, trade goods, hold council meetings, and participate in ceremonies. Hundreds of tipis were set up in a huge camp. Men and women who were ready to marry were introduced at these summer reunions, and people were free to switch bands or start new ones.

Camp chiefs

Each camp had **chiefs**, or leaders, who were wise and experienced men. They were trusted and admired and expected to be generous, loyal, honorable, and brave. People in a camp listened to the wise words of their chiefs and typically followed their advice.

Guilds and societies

Some men and women in Plains camps belonged to clubs called **guilds** or **societies**. The members had **social status**, or importance, in their village. Most men's societies were for hunting and warfare. Women belonged to farming and craft guilds. They met and worked together to help one another accomplish tasks or create beautiful and useful works of art. Not all members belonged to the same band, so the members from different camps met at the summer reunions.

The warrior society

Warrior societies grew after horses came to the Plains. Men devoted more time to warfare because they could travel farther and make quick getaways on horseback. Sometimes they held contests in which they tried to get close enough to an enemy to humiliate him by touching him with a stick or stealing his horses. Recording these humiliations was called "counting **coups**," or hits.

Plains police

At the summer gathering of bands, one warrior society was appointed police force for the year. The men who belonged to that society supervised the buffalo hunts of their camp, stopped people from hunting the buffalo too early, mediated fights, and made sure punishments were carried out within and outside the camp. Warrior societies also gave food and horses to anyone in need.

HUNTING THE BUFFALO

The buffalo was an important source of food, clothing, shelter, tools, and weapons. Every part of the buffalo was used. The meat was eaten fresh or dried and made into hard strips called **jerky**. The **hide**, or skin, of the buffalo was used to make clothing, blankets, and tipis. Horns and bones were made into tools, cups, and weapons.

Native hunters had to be creative to catch buffalo because it was difficult to get close to these huge animals without scaring them away. In winter, hunters approached buffalo mired in deep snow and shot them on the spot with their arrows. Sometimes hunters covered themselves in animal hides and crept up to the buffalo. They tried to drive their spears into an animal, hoping to make a kill before the herd ran away.

The buffalo jump

Before the hunters had horses, hunting buffalo on foot with handmade spears and arrows resulted in only a few animals being killed at a time. A clever method known as a **buffalo jump** could trap and kill many buffalo at once. Hunters created a V-shaped pathway of large stones that led toward a cliff. They wore animal skins over their head and shoulders to disguise themselves. They scared the herd to create a stampede, causing the panicked buffalo to run over the cliff.

With the help of horses

When horses came to the plains, hunters were able to travel much farther and faster, and hunting became much easier. Hunters on horseback could guide a large herd and drive them over a buffalo jump, or they could ride along with a herd to kill the buffalo.

Charging into the herd!

Hunting buffalo by charging into the herd required great courage and skill. Before a hunt, a few **scouts** rode ahead to assess the size of the herd. After the scouts gave the signal, the other hunters prepared their spears and arrows and charged toward the buffalo. They surrounded a group and attacked from all sides, dodging swiftly among the buffalo on their horses. They shot only as many animals as they needed.

Collecting the hunt

When the hunt was finished and the rest of the herd had run away, the band collected the slain buffalo. Each hunter had identifying marks on his arrows and spears, allowing him to claim the animals he had killed. The women at the nearby camp removed the skins of the buffalo and cut up the meat.

Hunters on horseback needed to ride while shooting arrows with both hands. Those who lost their balance were trampled by the heavy buffalo.

FOODS FROM THE LAND

Some Plains nations were farmers who stayed in one location and grew crops such as corn, beans, squash, sunflowers, and pumpkins. They went on hunting trips only a few times a year. Other nations were strictly hunters.

These nomadic people also collected wild berries and root vegetables wherever they could. Hunting bands often visited farming villages to trade buffalo meat for vegetables. People who lived near the woodland areas of the plains also hunted and ate other animals such as deer, elk, turkey, and quail.

The main food source

The main source of food for a Plains camp was buffalo meat. After a buffalo hunt, people ate as much cooked meat as they could. They dried the rest and saved it for times when they would not have fresh meat to eat. It only took a few days for meat to dry in the sun and become jerky, which lasted for months. Sometimes the **curing**, or preserving, process was speeded up by smoking the meat over a fire.

Favorite foods

A favorite meal in a Plains camp was a stew made of vegetables and buffalo meat. Another was a sausage dish made by stuffing meats and kidney suet into a cleansed buffalo intestine.

The intestines themselves could be roasted until they were crispy and then eaten like chips. Buffalo blood was made into a thick, jelly-like pudding. Smoked buffalo tongue was considered a delicacy.

Pemmican

Some meat was made into **pemmican**, which lasted a long time. Pemmican was made by drying buffalo meat and then pounding it with a stone into a paste that was mixed with fat and berries. This mixture was shaped into cakes. People could survive for weeks on jerky and pemmican alone.

Soups and stews were cooked by heating rocks over a fire and then dropping them into a rawhide case filled with water.

HIDES AND BONES

© Howard Terpning

The people of the Plains did not waste a single part of the buffalo they hunted. The hide of the buffalo became tipis, clothing, drums, shields, and bedding. Bones were used to make toboggans, tools, weapons, and utensils. Even the brains and liver of the buffalo were useful!

Cleaning the hide

After the hunters killed the buffalo, the women of the camp stripped off the hides. They stretched the hides out flat on a rock or rack, held them down with pegs and carefully scraped off the fat and gristle. When the hides were clean, the women soaked them until the fur could be removed with a scraper.

Buffalo robes

To make winter buffalo **robes**, the fur was left on the hide, and the robes were worn fur-side in. People also used the robes as covers or mattresses. Sometimes men painted pictures on their robes to show dreams they had or to tell a story. The fur robe shown here talks of guns, horses, and battles.

Tanning a hide

Tanning is the process that turns an animal hide into soft leather so it can be used to make clothes and bags. To tan a hide, women rubbed a liquid into it to soften and preserve it. Sometimes this liquid was made from the brains and liver of the buffalo. The women stretched the hides next to a fire pit of rotted cottonwood or other plants. The smoke from the fire gave the leather a gold or brown color, kept it soft, and helped repel insects.

The buffalo skins were stretched tightly and scraped clean of fat and gristle. They were left to dry in the sun.

Rawhide

Rawhide is a stiff, hard leather. It was made by cleaning and soaking the buffalo skin and then drying it in the sun. Native people used rawhide for things that provided protection, such as shields or the soles of moccasins.

Rawhide was also used to make drumheads. It was soaked and stretched. After it was dry, it held its shape and was rubbed with oils to make it more flexible.

(left) Buffalo horns were used to make spoons.

(right) Toboggans were made by tying buffalo ribs together.

This shield was made of buffalo rawhide and decorated with eagle feathers.

Some tipis were so large that it took 50 hides to make one!

17

MEN'S CLOTHING

Clothing was made from tanned buffalo hides. Plains people also used the skins of other animals such as deer, elk, and moose. The styles of clothing differed from nation to nation, especially in the types of decorations and accessories that were used.

Breechcloths and leggings

When the weather was warm, men and boys dressed lightly. They wore **breechcloths** or **aprons**. A breechcloth was a long strip of soft leather that went between the legs and under a belt and then draped over it. An apron was made of two panels of leather that were tied to a belt and hung down in the front and back. In cooler weather, both men and women wore ponchos or shirts and fur robes. On their legs, men and boys wore leggings made of long tubes of leather that were attached to their belts. Leggings kept legs warm and protected them from scrapes and cuts. **Moccasins** were worn on the feet.

The man in this picture is wearing an apron and leggings. Both the leggings and apron are held up by a belt.

© James Bama

Regalia

Men's clothing was often decorated with feathers or fur items. These decorated articles of clothing are called **regalia**. Men's regalia consisted of items that showed the military rank or achievements of the wearers. Some showed their membership in a society. These special items were worn in ceremonies and in battles, to protect the wearer from harm. Regalia items included belts, shields, breastplates, bear-claw or porcupine-quill necklaces, lances, and headdresses, such as the buffalo headdress on the right.

*(above) This Comanche warrior wears a feather **bonnet** and carries a shield and lance.*

(right) This Arapaho warrior is wearing a choker and breastplate made of carved beads.

(right) The Crow greased their bangs to stand straight up. The painted sleeves of their colorful outfits were decorated with long fringes.

19

GIRLS' AND WOMEN'S CLOTHES

Plains women wore simple leather dresses that tied at the shoulders. Extra leather could be attached to the dresses to make a cape or long sleeves for cooler weather. The clothes were made from buffalo hide, elk hide, or deer hide. Women often wore belts from which they hung leather pouches that contained useful items such as knives, flint, and sewing awls.

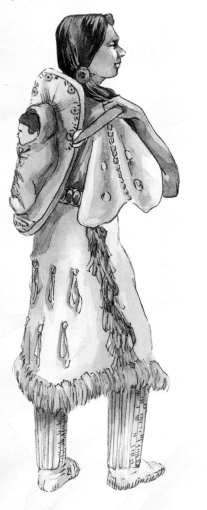

© Howard Terpning

(left) A Plains woman is carrying her baby in a cradleboard on her back. She wears knee-high moccasins. (right) This Sioux woman wears a buckskin dress decorated with long fringes, beads, and tiny bells. A beaded yoke covers her shoulders. She carries her husband's war shield to show her pride in his bravery in battle.

Girls wore the same styles of clothing as that of their mothers.

(left) Women wore buffalo robes to stay warm in winter.

(right) This Plains woman wears a combination of Plains styles. Her dress has long fringes and blue beads. She wears a belt with metal disks and carries an eagle feather, which is considered sacred.

MEN'S ROLES AND DUTIES

Men were expected to protect and provide for their families and bands. They were brought up to be expert hunters, and they trained the boys in their band to make weapons and tools, to ride well, and to track animals. Men were also responsible for defending their bands from attacks by wild animals or enemies.

Scouting was an important skill for both hunting and warfare. There were no telephones in those days, so scouts provided information and warnings. They located animals for hunting, found places where fruits and vegetables were growing, and escorted women there. They guarded the women and made sure they were safe.

These Comanche "wolf men" scouts are covering the tracks of their band's war party, which has crossed into enemy territory. Their headdress identifies them as part of their band's warrior society.

© Tom Lovell

Trading for goods

After European fur traders arrived in North America, many nations traded buffalo hides and other furs for useful items such as pots and pans, shovels, and other metal objects, which the native people did not make. They also traded for woven wool blankets and other fabrics, glass beads, sugar, coffee, mirrors, and rifles. Many Europeans traded only with men.

Making and decorating items

Men made the tools and weapons they used. They also took time to make and decorate their bonnets and other regalia with skins and feathers. They painted their shields and clothing and used quills or beads to decorate sacred items. Men also decorated their horses by braiding their manes or tails or by painting their coats with natural dyes.

THE MANY JOBS OF WOMEN

Women were busy from dawn until bedtime. They took care of their families and relatives and looked after the family home, which belonged to them. Women were in charge of setting up tipis when the band reached a new location and taking them down when they were ready to move again. Women also arranged the tipi furnishings.

Working together

Women worked together to complete many tasks. They gathered wild fruits and vegetables from the land and carried water from rivers or streams. They skinned, cleaned, and butchered the animals after a buffalo hunt. They made clothing and other items from buffalo hides. At some camps, women planted gardens in which they grew corn, beans, and squash. They harvested the crops, cooked the meals, and dried and stored the rest of the food for future use.

Men often prepared the fields for farming, but women tended the crops because they were considered closer to Grandmother Earth.

Craftspeople

Women were skilled craftspeople. They took great care in creating items for their relatives, such as baskets, containers, robes, cradleboards, and moccasins and decorated them with beads and quills. Their work was also traded for valuable items made by other nations and by Europeans. An intricately quilled buffalo robe, for example, could be traded for a horse! A woman who could produce many beautiful items was highly respected in her band.

Helping and sharing

Women helped one another in the camp. If a woman was expecting a baby, other women helped her do her work. If someone was ill, women brought food to the sick person. Everyone shared their food with elderly people who had no children.

Encouraging the family

An important part of a woman's duties was motivating her family. She praised her children for every effort they made or task they finished. Before a hunt or battle, women encouraged the men to be brave. They defended the children and elderly of the camp against animal or enemy attacks while the men were away. Some women were warriors who fought alongside the men, and some men did "women's" jobs.

© Howard Terpning

Children were considered members of their mother's clan. This mother made a cradleboard to carry her baby and keep him safe.

Women taught their daughters the things they needed to know to become good mothers. Both "mothers" look after their "babies."

EDUCATING THE CHILDREN

© Tom Lovell

Children in a Plains camp did not go to school. They learned by watching and imitating their parents and grandparents as they performed daily chores and tasks. Fathers, grandfathers, and uncles taught boys how to ride horses, hunt, and fight. Girls helped their mothers cook and dry food and sat with the older women to learn how to sew and decorate clothing. They made beautiful items to give away as gifts.

Teaching with stories

Listening to stories was another important part of learning for children. Since there were no books or written language, children learned about their families, ancestors, and the history of their nation by hearing stories over and over. Stories also provided lessons on behavior. Elders were often the storytellers.

Using special skills

Children in a Plains camp were encouraged to use their special talents. If they showed a particular ability or skill, they were given the opportunity to learn that skill from others who had similar talents. Children who had what we might consider handicaps were encouraged to do something they could do well. If a person could not walk, for example, he or she could learn to be a storyteller.

Becoming adults

When children matured, ceremonies were held to show that they were becoming young men and women and were ready to take on more responsible roles in the community. At that time, they were given new names.

(right) A Cheyenne grandmother performs a ceremony for her granddaughter to show that she is now a young woman. (below) This mother gives her young children a lesson about nature.

© Howard Terpning

SPORTS AND GAMES

Games and sports were important in Native life. Children played games that helped them develop life skills. Some games involved thinking and guessing. Others imitated the future lives of boys and girls. For example, to practice becoming good mothers, girls played with dolls that they carried around on small cradleboards. They also put together tiny tipis so they would know how to set up a big one when they were older.

Hoop games

Boys played games, such as hoop and pole games, which helped them become hunters and warriors. Hoop and pole games allowed boys to practice shooting at moving targets. The hoops were made of flexible branches covered with rawhide. One player rolled the hoop in the direction of two other players, who tried to shoot their poles through the hoop as it rolled. Sometimes the boys scooted the poles along the ground to guess where the hoop would stop.

Team sports

Team games were considered good practice for warfare. Several games played by the Plains nations resembled the sports we play today, such as hockey and soccer. Shinny was a game much like hockey, in which players used curved sticks to hit a puck made out of a rawhide-covered stone. Players hit the puck across icy areas and through the opposing team's goalposts.

In the ancient game of lacrosse, players held long poles with rawhide pouches at the end. They caught and threw a ball to other team members. The playing area was sometimes miles long, and several hundred players could play at once. The rowdy players often hit, pushed, and tripped each other, letting out loud yelps as they charged!

In this lacrosse game, with players dressed alike, hundreds of men struggle to get control of the ball.

PRAYER AND GRATITUDE

Most Native people considered all life to be sacred. Each day they offered prayers for others and expressed gratitude for everything in their lives. They thought of the Earth as the Grandmother of all life and the Creator as the Grandfather. People also gave thanks to the sun, moon, and the winds in the four directions. They understood that they shared the earth with animals, plants, and rocks. When hunting an animal, they asked its permission beforehand and thanked it for sacrificing its life. They did not waste any part of an animal they killed.

Seeking a vision

Before becoming men, boys sometimes went out into the wilderness and stayed alone, cold, and hungry, in order to pray for a deeper understanding of life. Sometimes they received spiritual messages about their future. The boy in the picture below has gone to a sacred place to pray. He has brought a buffalo skull with him to help him seek spiritual guidance from the spirits of the buffalo. The rock formation behind him also resembles a giant buffalo skull.

© Tom Lovell

GLOSSARY

apron Two panels of leather that were tied to a belt and worn by men and boys

band A group of people who lived together in a camp

bonnet A headdress decorated with items such as feathers, beads, and porcupine quills

breechcloth A long piece of soft leather that was worn by men and boys and looped under and over a belt; similar to an apron

buffalo jump A method of hunting in which a herd of buffalo were caused to stampede over a cliff by hunters

ceremony A formal act or ritual performed following customs or a set of actions as in a wedding

clan A group of people who are related by a common ancestor

coup A humiliation, such as being touched by an enemy's stick or having horses stolen

Great Plains A huge grassland region located in the central part of North America

hide The skin of an animal

jerky Strips of meat, especially buffalo or beef, which were dried in the sun

lacrosse A team sport of Native American origin in which players, using long-handled sticks with a webbed pouch on their end, try to get a ball into the opposing team's goal

lodge A type of dwelling; a home

moccasins Shoes made of soft leather

nation A large group of people who share the same origins, customs, laws, leaders, and, sometimes, language

nomadic Describing people who have no permanent home but move from place to place, as in hunters who follow buffalo herds

pemmican A food made of dried strips of buffalo meat that have been pounded into paste, mixed with fruit, and shaped into cakes

plain A grassy area of land

Plains Referring to the geographic area of the Great Plains or the animals or people who lived there

poncho A blanket-like cloak with a hole for the head

rawhide Stiff leather used to make moccasins, shields, or drumheads

regalia Highly-decorated clothing or items worn for ceremonies and other special occasions

robe A buffalo hide with the fur left on that was used as a winter coat or bedding and was sometimes painted with pictures

scout A person who explores carefully or spies to obtain information about animals, landscape, or the position of enemies

stampede To cause animals to run in a panic, as in over a cliff

tanning A process of making leather from the hides of animals by soaking them in a solution and drying and stretching them

travois A French name for a device made of two long poles that were attached to a horse or dog and used to transport belongings

tribe A group of families, clans, or bands who share common ancestry, culture, and leaders

vision A dream experience following prayer, fasting, and being alone, which results in a deeper understanding of life

warrior society A club whose members take part in acts of war, mediate fights, patrol areas, and help those who need assistance

INDEX

2 3 4 5 6 7 8 9 0 Printed in the U.S.A. 0 9 8 7 6 5 4 3 2